LANCASHIRE BUSES IN THE 1980S

GEORGE FAIRBAIRN

AMBERLEY

First published 2018

Amberley Publishing
The Hill, Stroud
Gloucestershire, GL5 4EP

www.amberley-books.com

Copyright © George Fairbairn, 2018

The right of George Fairbairn to be identified
as the Author of this work has been asserted in
accordance with the Copyrights, Designs and
Patents Act 1988.

ISBN 978 1 4456 7056 0 (print)
ISBN 978 1 4456 7057 7 (ebook)

British Library Cataloguing in Publication Data.
A catalogue record for this book is available from
the British Library.

Origination by Amberley Publishing.
Printed in the UK.

Introduction

At the start of the 1980s I took up employment in Rochdale, in the north-west of England, and over the following years I took my camera with me in the car or on my bicycle. Business and family commitments competed for my time; however, I was able to get a photographic sample of the bus scene in Rochdale and more widely in Lancashire in the momentous years up to and immediately after deregulation in 1986. These are some of those photographs.

On account of opportunity rather than inclination, I took many more in Rochdale than elsewhere in Lancashire. I have done my best to try to make an allowance for that and present a more balanced geographical view, so I apologise to anyone whose favourite local operator does not appear in these images – this omission is not for want of motivation.

I have chosen to interpret the concept of Lancashire as that of the former county before the creation of the metropolitan authorities. At the time of these photographs towns like Rochdale and Oldham, which were in Greater Manchester, still had Lancashire postal addresses and a good proportion of their inhabitants still looked upon themselves as Lancastrians. I have not included photographs of Manchester or Liverpool operators in their home cities.

My thanks are due in particular to my son Andrew. As a baby, strapped to my chest in a sling, he involuntarily accompanied on many of these photographic expeditions. His forbearance is much appreciated. I am also indebted to Brian Girling, whose website, www.buslistsontheweb.co.uk, has been an invaluable resource, and who has kindly cleared up some difficulties in vehicle identification for me.

Blackburn Transport 131 (LFR 131T), a Dennis Dominator with locally constructed East Lancashire bodywork, pulls away from Accrington Market. The bus was later sold to Rennies, Dunfermline.

Blackburn Transport 69 (KBV 49F), a Leyland Atlantean PD1 with an East Lancs body. When new it had a somewhat smaller destination aperture.

Accrington bus station plays host to Blackburn Coachlines 310 (NHL 260X), a Plaxton Supreme-bodied Leyland Leopard PSU5D/4R, which was new to National Travel East in 1981 and originally registered LHE 260W.

Another second-hand coach acquisition by Blackburn Coachlines was FUT 6V, a Plaxton Supreme-bodied Leyland Leopard PSU3E/4R. It was supplied new to Leicester City Transport in 1979 and was purchased by Blackburn in 1986. It is seen arriving in Manchester on the 701 service from Blackburn.

Blackburn 101 (JFR 401N), a 1975 Leyland Atlantean AN68 with an East Lancs body, is seen in the town in the 1982 version of the livery.

The Dennis Dominator found little favour with Blackburn Transport. One of only seven bought, East Lancs-bodied 5 (DBV 5W) was delivered in an unusual blue livery advertising Blackburn's 'Easi-Fare' ticket. By the mid-1980s this had been replaced by a green and white advertisement for the countywide Lancashire Bus Pass.

Blackburn Transport 172 (HTD 323K) passes under the Lancashire & Yorkshire Railway's bridge on Darwen Street, Blackburn. The Bristol RESL/East Lancs was new to Darwen Corporation and, after being sold by Blackburn Transport, it saw further service with Barry's Coaches, Weymouth and Metrowest, in whose fleet it acquired the name 'The Highwayman'.

New as Darwen Corporation 4, STC 890L was another Bristol RESL/East Lancs, but this time with a different style of grille. Seen here as Blackburn Transport's 176, it passed to East Staffordshire District Council and then to Stevenson's of Uttoxeter and Astill's of Leicester. Behind is Ex-Leicester Bristol RESL/East Lancs 150 (LJF 5F).

Wearing another version of the Blackburn livery, 6 (OCW 6X), a Leyland AN68C/1R with an
East Lancs body, loads in Accrington for a return trip to its home town.

Blackpool Transport 515 (HFR 515E) was a Leyland Titan PD3A/1 with MCCW bodywork,
and is seen here in the operator's yard. It had an unexpected further life as a trainer with
London & Country and ended its days as a donor vehicle for others of its type, being owned by
the Lancastrian Transport Trust.

Another similar bus to become a trainer was Blackpool 534 (LFT 534F), which is seen here on Drake Street, Rochdale.

Post-deregulation, Blackpool Transport was one of a number of operators to tempt passengers with the retro delights of former London Transport RMs. 530 (ALD 989B), formerly London Transport RM1989 of 1964 vintage, was acquired in April of 1988. It is seen operating on Blackpool Promenade. Withdrawn by Blackpool in 1996, it was purchased by Reading Mainline the following year.

Blackpool Transport 549 (E549 GFR) was an Optare City Pacer – one of the first designs of minibus to show that these little vehicles, whatever their other shortcomings might be, could look attractive and didn't have to resemble vans with windows.

A pair of smart East Lancs-bodied Leyland Atlanteans, such as graced many a Lancashire municipal fleet, Blackpool Transport 322 (URN 322V) and 350 (GHG 350W) await service at the company's depot. 322, its upper deck windows panelled over, became a driver trainer in later life.

A pair of Blackpool's AEC Swifts. Nearer the camera is 562 (UFR 562K) in the livery applied to these buses. New in 1971, it was withdrawn in August 1983. Its more remote stablemate, 577 (OFR 577M), new in 1974, survived until March 1987. It wears the later livery with green roof and waistband.

In 1973, Burnley, Colne & Nelson Joint Transport Committee bought five Leyland Nationals. Less than a year later, after local government reorganisation, they became the property of Burnley & Pendle. An example is seen here in their livery in 1981.

Eight Bristol RELL6Gs with distinctive MCW bodies were bought new by Sunderland Corporation in 1969 and then purchased from their successor, Tyne & Wear PTE, by Burnley & Pendle at the end of the 1970s. 98 (JBR 105F), which had been converted to single-door, fifty-seat configuration by Burnley & Pendle, loads up in Burnley bus station. It later passed to Phillips of Shiptonthorpe.

Another immigrant from Tyneside to Burnley & Pendle, Leyland National 24 (HNL 160L) is seen here laying over in Burnley. After deregulation it was operated by SUT, Sheaf Line and Compass Bus.

Another of Burnley & Pendle's eclectic collection of single-deckers in the early 1980s was 85 (LHG 385H), a Northern Counties-bodied Bristol RESL. It was later purchased by Silver Service, Middleton.

YHG 15V, 15 in the Burnley & Pendle fleet, was a Leyland Leopard PSU4E/4R new in 1980. On withdrawal it was sold to Bluebird, Middleton, who replaced the dual-purpose Alexander Y-type body seen here with an East Lancs bus body in 1996 and re-registered it as MAZ 4969. It was still in existence, in the guise of a cafe, at a farm shop near Bristol in 2016.

Another of Burnley & Pendle's unusual second-hand purchases was 199, an Alexander-bodied Bristol VRT new to Tayside Transport. It carries a double-deck version of Burnley & Pendle's coach livery and had been retrofitted with coach seating.

New to Burnley & Pendle in 1976 was 157 (URN 157R), an East Lancs-bodied Bristol VRT, which is seen here in Burnley bus station. Its subsequent owners included Hogg, Boston and Brylaine Travel, Coningsby.

Representing the most customary conventional choice of coachbuilder on a Bristol chassis, ECW-bodied VRT 165 (FFR 165S) waits at Burnley. Later lives saw it with Green, Kirkintilloch, Kelvin Central, Nottingham Omnibus and South Gloucester Bus & Coach.

The resolutely rectilinear style of the P-type Alexander body on Burnley & Pendle's Volvo B10M 62 (E62 JFV) draws the attention of a bystander as it approaches Burnley bus station. Burnley & Pendle's sale to Stagecoach saw the bus pass to Stagecoach Ribble and then to their Midland Red Slough subsidiary.

Burnley & Pendle also bought some Alexander-bodied Volvo deckers at the same time as 62, above. 101 (E101 JFV), an RV-bodied B10M-50, passed with the undertaking to Stagecoach, and thence to Blazefield with the further sale of the company in 2001. Stagecoach had not seen the last of this bus though; Blazefield later sold it to Lincolnshire Road Car, which itself was subsequently purchased by Stagecoach. Perhaps exhausted by all these manoeuvres, this bus went for scrap in 2009.

As well as big buses, Burnley & Pendle invested in minibuses in the late 1980s. 86 (E86 HRN) was a Robin Hood-bodied Mercedes-Benz 811D. These little buses bore the brand name 'Whizzard', and among other duties found themselves operating the Centreline city centre service in Manchester on Sundays – the tender for which was won after deregulation by Burnley & Pendle.

In 1986, Burnley & Pendle acquired the business of Sandown of Padiham, who used the fleet name of Viscount Central. The name was used on Burnley & Pendle's coach fleet, as seen here on Jonkhere Jubilee-bodied Volvo B10M-61 D202 VBV, which is parked at the excursion stand at Burnley and advertising various Continental trips.

Burnley & Pendle 141 (YCW 141N) passed to SUT and found itself working for Yelloway, of Rochdale, in 1987. By this time SUT and Yelloway were in common ownership.

Another Viscount Central coach, VFV 7V, a Leyland Leopard PSU3E/4R with a Duple Dominant body, waits at Rochdale bus station, with the driver catching up on the news.

Standard fare for Lancashire municipal buses in the seventies and eighties was the East Lancs-bodied Bristol RE, and a Burnley & Pendle example was 149 (YCW 849N), which is seen here in Accrington. A subsequent owner was Ogden's of St Helens.

Burnley & Pendle 53 (YHG 3N), a Duple Dominant-bodied Leyland Leopard, was loaned for some time to Southend Transport when new, and retained that operator's livery with Burnley & Pendle fleet names upon its return north. Resale took it across the Pennines to Hunter, Seaton Delaval.

Another vehicle loaned to Southend was 13 (WRN 13R), an Alexander AY-type-bodied Leyland Leopard that was photographed in Rochdale. In the early 1990s it passed to Glenstuart Travel of Wolverhampton.

Ellen Smith A886 DND, a Plaxton Paramount 3200-bodied Leyland Tiger, awaits a load outside the attractively curved façade of the Wheatsheaf Hotel, Littleborough. This coach became OIB 3604 in the Rossendale coach fleet after their purchase of the Rochdale coach operator in 1991.

Sporting a rather anachronistic Leyland badge, Ellen Smith's Leopard YDK 165L awaits further duties at the operator's yard. It later passed to Border Coaches.

FHG 592S started life as a Leyland development vehicle, B15.02. Built in 1975, it was eventually registered in 1977 – the year I remember seeing it in Greater Glasgow PTE colours at the Scottish Motor Show. By then the model had been named the Titan TN15 and this vehicle undertook extensive demonstration duties over several years before being purchased by Fishwick of Leyland, a frequent collector of unusual Leyland buses. Here it is seen soon after they bought it, still in demonstrator livery and wearing two fleet numbers.

Fishwick 14 (PCK 193P) was a Leyland National 11351/1R, new to Fishwick's in 1976. The green livery of the independent contrasts with the massed ranks of red Nationals of Ribble at Preston bus station.

A462 LFV, at first glance an ECW-bodied Leyland Olympian, was in fact a Leyland Atlantean AN69 constructed as a left-hand drive chassis for export. It was then converted to right-hand drive before bodying in the then-current Olympian style by ECW and was subsequently purchased by Fishwick, Leyland. It gave many years of service and is now preserved.

A more conventional decker in the Fishwick fleet was 22 (SRN 103P), an East Lancs-bodied Leyland Atlantean AN68. After sale by Fishwicks it served for several years as an exhibition bus for the Royal Zoological Society of Scotland, covered in a wrap featuring images of various exotic species.

Fishwick 23 (GRN 895W) was the only other AN69 to enter passenger service in the UK. This bore the more conventional ECW body style for the Atlantean, except for the rear bustle, which accommodated noise-suppression equipment of the kind fitted to the B20 Fleetlines of London Transport. The chassis was built in 1975 but was not registered until 1981.

Fylde's 30 (ARN 808C) was new to Ribble in 1965. It was one of three Weymann-bodied Leyland Leopard PSU3/3s that passed to Fylde in 1979. Withdrawn in 1982, it was bought by the *Blackpool Gazette*, who removed the panelling and glazing from the rear and the last two bays on each side and ran it for a few years, describing it as a 'fun bus'.

Fylde Borough Transport 48 (STC 48L) was a Pennine-bodied Seddon Pennine RU, one of six delivered to Lytham St Annes in 1972.

Fylde 77 (ATD 281J) was one of Lytham's first batch of Leyland Atlanteans with a Northern Counties body of a distinctive style similar to examples for Nottingham Corporation. New in 1968, it survived into Blackpool Transport ownership. It has since been acquired for preservation by the Lancastrian Transport Trust.

A later incarnation of the Leyland Atlantean/Northern Counties combination with Fylde was 84 (OCK 84P). In many ways the body was similar to the Greater Manchester Standard. This bus was refurbished by Northern Counties in 1992 and gained a Palatine I style front, subsequently being re-registered SIB 8405.

LFV 309 was a Metro-Cammell-bodied Leyland Titan PD2/21 that was new to Blackpool Corporation in 1965. It was purchased by the neighbouring Lytham municipality in 1970 and served them for many years, latterly, as seen here, in the guise of a trainer.

Another local operator to provide second-hand vehicles for Lytham was Merseyside PTE. This 1964 vintage Leyland Atlantean PDR 1/1 has a Metro-Cammell body in the distinctive style of its original owner, Liverpool Corporation.

Halton Borough Council 20 (ACW 920R) was a Leyland National purchased new in 1977. It spent much of its time in all-over advertising liveries, such as this one for a local motor factors.

RTC 645L bore the fleet number 1 in the Halton fleet, and is seen here arriving on the Lancashire side of the Silver Jubilee Bridge, which spans the Mersey between Runcorn and Widnes. The bridge replaced an earlier transporter bridge, and at the time of writing is itself being superseded by the new Mersey Gateway crossing. This bus was the first Leyland National delivered to a municipal operator – Halton's predecessor Widnes, in whose colours it is now preserved.

As with so many Lancashire municipal operators, Halton purchased East Lancashire-bodied Bristol REs in the 1970s. 10 (MCK 210P) was an RELL6G with a dual-door body and dual-purpose seats.

A more unusual East Lancs body was built on the Leyland Leopard PSU3B/4R chassis of Halton's 8 (JFV 294N). Only three examples of this style of East Lancs body were built: this specimen and the identical 9 (JFV 295N) for Halton, both of which were re-bodied in 1983 with a more conventional East Lancs bus body; and Hyndburn's Seddon Pennine RU STC 986M.

A Hyndburn Transport Leyland Leopard PSU 4E/2R with an East Lancs body, 45 (EHG 45S) is seen in Accrington town centre.

Again in Accrington, here is Hyndburn Transport 31 (OTF 358K), a Bristol RESL/East Lancs, which was new to Accrington Corporation. It was eventually converted to a Mobile Ticket Information Office.

Hyndburn 38 (STC 986M) was the unique East Lancs coach-bodied Seddon Pennine RU. Only two other examples of this body were built, both on Leopard chassis for Halton. These latter examples were re-bodied with more conventional bus bodies by East Lancs in 1983 and were subsequently sold, ironically enough, to Hyndburn. One of those has been preserved; 38, however, was delicensed in 1985.

A Seddon Pennine RU with more conventional East Lancs body was Hyndburn 37 (BTF 377L), which is seen here in Accrington bus station.

Accrington bus station finds Hyndburn 177 (HFT 177K), an East Lancs-bodied Leyland Atlantean PDR1A/1 that was new to Accrington Corporation, laying over.

Blackburn Boulevard bus station is the background to Hyndburn 103 (SCW 103X), an East Lancs-bodied Dennis Dominator that was new in 1982. An accident in 1986 cost this vehicle its roof and repairs included a new dome lacking the distinctive peak. The bus was sold to Chester City Transport in August 1980.

Hyndburn's 105 (A105 KN), an East Lancs-bodied Dennis Dominator, was new in 1983 and had clearly been the beneficiary of a recent repaint when seen in this 1987 view. The bus later passed to Chester City Transport, that inveterate collector of other municipalities' cast-off Dominators.

Hyndburn's Duple Dominant-bodied Leyland Leopard had a colourful career. New to City of Oxford Motor Services in 1978 as LWL 5S, it was involved in an accident in February of the next year and the coach was fitted with a replacement body identical to the original. Hyndburn purchased the vehicle in 1987 and subsequently re-registered it, as seen here.

An exceptionally well-travelled member of the Hyndburn fleet was 51 (B51 XFV). This unusual East Lancs-bodied Dennis Falcon H was new in 1985 and, along with similar 50 (A50 LHG), passed with the undertaking to Stagecoach in 1996. Both Falcons were sold to South Lancs Travel the following year, and thence were acquired by Arriva North West. B51 XFV returned to Accrington as part of Pilkington's fleet and was subsequently sold to an operator in Malta, where it was registered FBY 768 and continued to give service until the controversial reorganisation of the island's bus services in 2011.

As many operators did in the mid-1980s, Hyndburn also embraced minibuses. This Ford Transit, 12 (C212 MCW), had the added luxury of dual-purpose seating on its body, built not, sadly, by MCW – that would have been too much of a coincidence! – but by Carlyle on a Dormobile frame. The passenger is about to demonstrate the difficulties in boarding or alighting with a pushchair in those far-off pre-low floor days.

If an MCW minibus was what you wanted in Accrington, then Hyndburn could supply those as well. 26 (E26 GCK), a Metrorider of 1987, awaits departure from Accrington for Blackburn.

Perhaps more interesting than it seems at first glance, Hyndburn Freight Rover Sherpa 22 (D512 NDA) was new to West Midlands PTE for its Sutton Coldfield 'Hail and Ride' network. Its eighteen-seat Carlyle body was fitted with an external light on the nearside of the front dome, which, when lit, indicated that the minibus was on the Hail and Ride part of the service. This light, now superfluous, lasted with the vehicle throughout the rest of its life with Hyndburn and subsequently with GHA Coaches of Wrexham.

Hyndburn, in common with other fleets in and around Greater Manchester, took advantage of the decision of the conurbation's PTE to shed a substantial number of buses at the start of deregulation in 1986. Ex-GMPTE KDB 688P became 130 with its new owners. GMPTE specified a three-box destination display and Hyndburn solved the problem of what to do with the extra real estate on the front of the Northern Counties body by applying the fleet number in a most unusual location. The Atlantean AN68, of 1975 vintage, later passed to Sheffield Omnibus.

Lancashire meets Yorkshire: Hyndburn Leyland Leopard/East Lancs EHG 44S, on hire to Sports Tours, Rochdale, is passed by Yorkshire Rider 7117 (WUM 117S), a Roe-bodied Leyland Fleetline.

One of Lancaster City Council's smart Alexander Y-type dual-purpose Leyland Leopards, MFR 17P, drives along Marine Road West in Morecambe.

Lancaster took an early opportunity to try out the Leyland National, taking three in late 1973 and early 1974. All three (including PTC 124M) were sold to Fishwick, Leyland, and 122/4 later joined Yeowart's of Whitehaven.

Preston bus station looms large in the background of this picture of Borough of Preston 108 (GBV 108N), a 1975 Leyland Atlantean AN68 with an Alexander dual-door body. In 1990 it became 212 in the Hyndburn fleet.

Because they were adjacent to the Leyland factory, Preston were well situated to make use of Leyland demonstrators when available. An example is VCW 85V, a Plaxton Supreme-bodied Leopard PSU3F/5R – the first Leopard to be fitted with a ZF gearbox, which it trumpets proudly on the side. After demonstration duties ended, the coach was sold to Mercer of Longridge.

Preston 219 (KRN 219H) was a Marshall-bodied Leyland Panther PSUR1A/1R – one of seven such dual-door builds new in 1970.

Preston also purchased second-hand Marshall-bodied Panthers. 239 (AUE 311J), also a PSUR1A/1, was one of five similar buses delivered to Midland Red in 1970 after they had taken over Stratford Blue, the independent that had ordered them. After Preston this bus operated for North Cornwall Cars and then Blair & Palmer of Carlisle.

Preston 344 (PHG 244P) was a Bristol LHS with an unusually narrow Duple Dominant coach body with bus seats. Later in life it became part of the Busways fleet.

Preston's response to the United Buses Zippy minibus fleet included 60 (D760 YCW), which was a Northern Counties-bodied Renault S56. It was one of twenty new in the spring of 1987. Horrocks of Brockton, Shropshire, were subsequent owners of this bus.

Preston 1 (DRN 1Y), a Leyland Atlantean AN68D/2R with East Lancs coach-seated body, heads through the town centre in 1987. It was re-registered XEC 415Y in 2000, the same year it was purchased for further service by P&O Lloyd of Bagillt before being exported to Ireland in 2003.

A Ribble Leyland Titan PB3/5 with MCW bodywork, 828 (TCK 828) passes St George's Hall, Liverpool. The similar 1775 (RCK 920) is preserved by the Ribble Vehicle Preservation Trust.

Ex-GMPTE 7093 (WBN 971L) became part of the Ribble fleet in the aftermath of deregulation. The driver takes in the latest news before setting off on the return trip to Bolton in this Park Royal-bodied Leyland Atlantean AN68. Subsequently transferred to the Bee Line fleet, it was sold in 1990 to Pennine Blue, Guide Bridge.

Another second-hand addition to the Ribble fleet was GDR 201N, an ex-Plymouth Citybus Leyland Atlantean AN68 with a different style of front panel. The centre door has received a somewhat ersatz modification.

A further ex-GMPTE bus to join Ribble was Park Royal-bodied Leyland Atlantean AN68 1642 (VNB 167L). By way of contrast it stands beside Greater Manchester Buses 8068 (BVR 68T), a Northern Counties-bodied Leyland Fleetline, which in due course operated on Merseyside as part of the Birkenhead & District operation of Greater Manchester Buses (South).

A stylish, if unusual addition to the Ribble fleet after deregulation was UHA 191H, an Alexander-bodied Daimler Fleetline CRG 6LXB new in 1969 to Midland Red. It and the following Park Royal-bodied Leyland Atlantean carry advertisements for the Greater Manchester multi-operator Clippercard.

Ribble's foray into the minibus market in the 1980s included 511 (D511 RCK), a 1986 Reeves-Burgess-bodied Mercedes-Benz L608D, which is seen in Accrington bus station at an early stage in its career.

Typical of the first wave of vehicles in the minibus revolution was Ribble's Freight Rover Sherpa with sixteen-seat Dormobile body, D588 VBV, which also operated the Hyndburn Circular service. Its modest size meant it had a good load on this 1987 journey.

A slightly later iteration of the minibus theme is seen in Ribble's 643 (E643 DCK), a Dormobile-bodied Renault S46.

Ribble Leyland Olympian 2113 (JFR 13W) takes a break on Chorlton Street, Manchester, before setting off to Nelson. This ECW-bodied bus of 1981 vintage had a long life, surviving with Shamrock, Poole, well into the first decade of the twenty-first century.

Ribble Leyland Olympian/ECW 2152 (B152 TRN) boasts an all-over advertisement commemorating a century of the *Lancashire Evening Post* at the Accrington bus station in 1987. It became a repeat offender in the all-over advertisement game, at various times wearing treatments for such enterprises as Travelwise, Hayes Garden Centres, Ambleside and Preston's Fishergate Shopping Centre. It gave many years of service with Ribble, Stagecoach and Blazefield Holdings.

DBV 833W, a Leyland National II of Ribble, stands at Burnley bus station while a group of passengers, clothed for the cold, windy, winter weather, await the opportunity to board.

A grimy Duple Laser-bodied Leyland Tiger of Ribble, B153 WRN stands at Burnley bus station. After the purchase of Ribble by Stagecoach, this coach was transferred north to the Cumberland fleet.

The ultimate in luxury provided by Ribble services in the 1980s is exemplified by 176, a Neoplan with relatively unusual Plaxton Paramount 4000 bodywork, which is seen here parked on Drake Street, Rochdale. Its subsequent owner, Amberline of Liverpool, operated in this same livery with the addition of their fleet name in black on the side between the front and middle axles.

Ex-Southdown Park Royal-bodied Leyland Atlantean AN68s PUF 142M and LCD 47P were other post-deregulation acquisitions by Ribble. They stand on a drizzly day on the Esplanade, Rochdale.

An early Leyland National in the Ribble fleet was 453 (NTC 632M). The Pay on Entry light is illuminated – a superfluous alert by the mid-1980s when driver-only operation was fairly ubiquitous in the area.

Ribble 1005 wore various colours with the fleet, including all-over white and National Holidays, but is here in the livery of the Sandpiper luxury coach unit. It is parked in Yelloway's coach station in Rochdale while on a National Express duplicate working. It saw further service with Tim's Travel, Sheerness, having been registered as MJI 8856.

Ribble Leyland Olympian/ECW 2125 (SCK 225X) lays over in Burnley bus station. This was another Olympian that was favoured with a variety of all-over advertisements.

Another draftee from Southdown, Leyland Atlantean AN68/Park Royal 1612 (PUF 142M) traverses Deansgate, Manchester.

In May 1989 Ribble was sold to Stagecoach. An early repaint into the corporate livery of its new owner was 1658 (JDB 115N), an ex-Greater Manchester Northern Counties-bodied Leyland Atlantean AN68 that was seen in Bolton bus station.

Ribble 640 (E640 DCK), a Dormobile-bodied Renault S46, wears a livery extolling a local insurance company in Bolton.

Ribble purchased the Beeline Buzz company in 1987 and cascaded some Ribble vehicles into the acquired fleet. Ribble buses operating Beeline services could be distinguished by their yellow front panels, as shown here on 394 (PTF 740L), an early Leyland National, which is parked near the city centre.

Subsequently, ex-Ribble vehicles in the Beeline fleet appeared fully painted in yellow with a red roof. One such was 708 (MRJ 271W), a Plaxton Supreme-bodied Leyland Leopard new to National Travel (West).

Ribble's post-deregulation fleet was bolstered by used acquisitions such as former Alexander (Fife) RXA 50J, an Alexander-bodied Daimler Fleetline. It is making its new allegiance very clear in Burnley bus station.

Taking up the sun at Bury interchange is Ribble 733 (UHG 733R), a Leyland National of 1976 vintage. Re-registered as YXI 2452, it crossed the Pennines when it joined the fleet of The Eden, West Auckland.

WFR 392V was originally a Leyland development vehicle built in 1978. At the end of 1979 it was loaned to Ribble, who allocated it fleet number 880. They subsequently renumbered it 686 and purchased it.

Ribble 382 (PTF 728L) was originally a dual-door Leyland National bus new in 1972; by the mid-1980s it had been converted to an information unit and is seen here at Christmas doing duty as part of a charitable appeal in Rochdale town centre. Subsequent owners provided it with an awning and it became a hospitality unit, bearing the name *Lady Dianne*.

Ribble's Duple Caribbean-bodied Leyland Tiger 135 (B135 ACK) turns into the approach to Burnley's bus station, with the embankment of the Leeds and Liverpool Canal in the background, to the left.

To alleviate a vehicle shortage in 1977, London purchased fourteen off-the-peg Bristol LHS6Ls. They were disposed of when their first Certificate of Fitness came due. TPJ 56S (BN56) was snapped up by Rossendale Transport in 1983 and was used until 1989 when it passed to Trimdon Motor Services. Here it is loading at Rossendale bus station.

One of the more startling advertising liveries to grace the streets was found on Rossendale Transport PRJ 485R, an ex-GMPT Northern Counties-bodied Daimler Fleetline that was new in 1976 and became part of the great cull of the GMPTE fleet that took place at the time of deregulation.

MTC 870K, an East Lancs-bodied Leyland Leopard of 1972, stands ready for duty in Yelloway's garage while on hire for its many stage services acquired under deregulation. It was new to Rossendale Joint Transport Committee.

It was not all one-way traffic from the former Greater Manchester Buses to Rossendale. Also seen on Yelloway's premises is Leyland Leopard/Plaxton GBO 285W. New to Hills, Tredegar, it was purchased in 1985 by Rossendale Transport and used on private hires, National Express duplicate work and the odd stage-carriage service. They re-registered it as LIB 1182. A subsequent sale saw it pass to Greater Manchester Buses (South) and when that operator was sold to Stagecoach, the bus gained their striped livery. In those colours it passed to the Cheshire Cheese Angling Club in Warrington, who had the benefit of it for many years.

Halton's two East Lancs coach-bodied Leyland Leopards, JFV 294/5N, received replacement bus bodies in 1983. Some of their coach seats, together with a twin-speed rear axle from a Ribble Leopard, found their way into refurbished Rossendale 5 (WTJ 905L). The bus, also with East Lancs body, was photographed in Rochdale bus station.

The murky mist of a wet Rochdale autumn day seems to suit the classic lines of Rossendale trainer 192 OTB. New to Haslingden Corporation in 1960, the East Lancs-bodied Leyland Titan PD2/40 became 44 in the Rossendale Transport fleet eight years later. It is now preserved in its original owner's blue and white livery.

Successor as trainer to 44 was Rossendale Leyland Titan PD3/4 XTJ 939D. Personally, I find that the 30-foot version of the East Lancs body has lost the elegance of proportion of its shorter antecedent.

YNA 356M was one of eleven Leyland and Daimler Fleetlines purchased from GMPTE by Rossendale as reinforcements for the fleet, which had acquired additional services following deregulation. 43, ex-GMPTE 7401, also debuted the Mark 1A style of body for GMPTE by Northern Counties, with a curved windscreen to improve visibility for the driver.

An attractive double-deck addition to the fleet in spring 1987 was 88, an East Lancs coach-seated Leyland Olympian, which is seen here when new while unloading outside Rochdale Town Hall. Later in its Rossendale career it became part of the Ellen Smith coach fleet, by that time owned by Rossendale. There it was re-registered as HIL 3188. By the mid-1990s it had passed to Rhondda Buses.

Former GMPTE 7434 (GND 500N) was the first bus to carry Rossendale's revised red cream and green livery, and proudly bears a prominent municipal crest on the front. The Daimler Fleetline/Northern Counties bus was 44 in its new fleet.

1988 brought four MCW Metroriders to the Rossendale fleet. 59 (E59 KHG) initially operated in this anonymous state but it was later acquired Handyrider fleetnames.

In addition to Metroriders bought as new, Rossendale Transport collected a number of others on the second-hand market. E519 YWF was new to Smith of Prenton in 1987 and found its way to the Lancashire municipal operator two years later.

Another post-deregulation second-hand purchase was 74 (ULS 318T), a 1979 Leyland Leopard PSU3/Alexander Y-type. It was subsequently sold to Blue Bus of Huddersfield, who operated it in a livery reminiscent of its original Alexander (Midland) scheme.

Gleaming in its new livery, ex-TMS BAJ 118Y loads at Rochdale bus station. It was one of three Leyland Tiger TRCTL11s with Duple Dominant bus bodywork that were acquired by Rossendale Transport from Trimdon Motor Services in 1988.

One of three Carlyle-bodied Freight Rover Sherpas new in 1986, 53 (D953 NOJ) lays over in Rochdale bus station.

OBN 504R was new to Lancashire United Transport and came to Rossendale Transport via Greater Manchester Buses. It was returned to Northern Counties for accident repair in 1988 and re-entered service with this rather lopsided appearance of its display.

One of four East Lancs-bodied Leyland Tigers purchased new by Rossendale Transport in 1989, 95 (F95 XBV) prepares to leave Rochdale and its drizzly rain for the intriguingly named Peppermint Bridge in Newhey.

Rossendale 49 (NTJ 808C) was an ex-Rawtenstall Leyland Leopard L1/East Lancs that was new in 1965. It is parked in the company of two new, unregistered Ford Cargos in 1984. It was subsequently purchased by Newhey ARLFC.

Among Rossendale's contributions to the minibus revolution was MCW Metro rider 56 (E56 KHG). It is photographed at the lengthy bus stand outside the operator's premises in Rawtenstall in full Handyrider livery.

Additional Caledonian infiltrators into the Rossendale fleet were a number of ex-Strathclyde PTE Leyland Atlanteans, such as 31 (KSU 857P), which is seen here in a begrimed condition at Rochdale bus station. It was new in 1975 as LA981 to Greater Glasgow PTE.

Stott's of Oldham ran a variety of second-hand vehicles on local stage services after deregulation. JAK 927N, a Roe-bodied Daimler Fleetline, was one of the last two new double-deckers acquired by Blue Ensign, Doncaster, in 1975, before the operator was purchased by South Yorkshire PTE.

In addition to buses, Stott's also had some coaches, such as MBU 821L, a Bedford YRQ of 1973 with Duple Dominant body. It is seen on hire to Yelloway, Rochdale, outside their Weir Street premises.

Another of Stott's ex-Yorkshire Fleetlines, in this case an Alexander-bodied example from West Yorkshire PTE that was new to Bradford Corporation. Commercial service 416 was introduced by Stott's in January 1987 and XAC was a regular performer on it.

Another ex-West Yorkshire PTE purchase by Stott's was JWU 254N, a Plaxton Derwent-bodied Leyland Leopard PSU4C/4R that is seen displaying somewhat ersatz destination equipment. Stott's later sold the bus to Central Coaches, Oldham.

Stott's took advantage of the local former PTE's sale of redundant vehicles, as did many operators in Lancashire and throughout the country. YNA 282M picks up a load in Oldham town centre.

SELNEC's Mark 1 standard double-deckers had a flat front windscreen but operating experience showed that the design of the windscreen deflected spray onto the exterior mirrors. YNA 303M was built with a curved screen to address this issue. Such was the success of the experiment that the modified windscreen was adopted for subsequent batches of bodies. In later life, YNA 303M stands on Oldham Road, Royton, while in the ownership of Stott's.

United Transport Limited operated minibuses in Preston under the Zippy fleet name. 060 (D368 SGB) was an Ivero 49.10 with Portuguese Elme bodywork. In the background is another Iveco, 001 (D410 FRV), with Robin Hood bodywork.

Another unusual vehicle in the Zippy fleet was 075 (E509 UNE), a Peugeot-Talbot Pullman with bodywork by TBP of Perry Bar, Birmingham.

Blue Bus of Eccles operated this Bristol RELH with an ECW coach body. It was new to Western National and had entered preservation, whereupon it was recalled to the standard and is seen in Manchester departing on service 15 to Culcheth.

E212 GNV was a Jonkhere-bodied DAF SB230, operated by Enterprise, Rochdale. It is photographed outside the Tom Mellor Ford dealership, part of the Mellor Group that included Mellor Coachcraft.

This fine vehicle was regularly to be found parked up on a side street in Rochdale in the 1980s. It was the transport of the Queensway Royals dance troop. New in May 1959, the Bedford SB3/ Yeates Europa C40F was first owned by Harwood of Bishop Auckland. Towards the end of its long life it was re-registered as ABV 617A and appears to have survived until 1995.

When SELNEC was formed in the late 1960s, it modified an order from the former Rochdale Corporation for Daimler Fleetlines. They received dual-door bodies by Northern Counties to SELNEC's standard design. As this was effectively an evaluation batch they were given fleet numbers in the EX series. TNB 759K was EX19, later becoming 6252. After sale by SELNEC's successor, Greater Manchester PTE, it spent many years in the ownership of the 16th Middleton Scout & Guide Band, in whose distinctive livery it is seen here. It is now owned by the SELNEC Preservation Society.

This attractive little coach, BOR 719J, was a Caetano-bodied Bedford VAS that was new to Castle, Waterlooville. In 1987 it is seen operating a stage service from Rochdale to Littleborough in the ownership of Bu-Val. Its entrance, behind the front axle, cannot have been the easiest arrangement for such a service, and quite how the driver collected the fares is not obvious.

The United Transport business in Greater Manchester, Bee Line Buzz Service, employed a number of Dodge S46s with Northern Counties bodywork to a style different from that purchased by the PTE and various other operators. D424 NNA is seen on driver familiarisation duties in Spotland.

Stockport Corporation were late adherents to the traditional rear-entrance half-cab double-decker, as seen here in the form of HJA 949E. The East Lancs-bodied Leyland Titan PD2/40 was originally Stockport 49, and by the time of this photograph it was in the custody of the Manchester Training Group of Middleton.

Citibus operated a service from Manchester to Middleton, where former Preston Marshall-bodied Leyland Panther KRN 221H loads up. It was later exported to the Isle of Man, becoming C58 MAN.

Harry Blundred's Thames Transit minibus operation ordered a substantial fleet of Ford Transits that were bodied in Rochdale by Mellor Coachcraft. Completed examples are seen here in the body-builder's yard, awaiting painting. In the background are Rochdale station and the dome of St John the Baptist Church.

SELNEC's original prototype Standard was PNF 941J (EX1, later 5466). Here it is parked in Rochdale while in the ownership of Father O'Leary of St Michael's, Oldham, who used it for school transport. It is now preserved and has been restored to its original condition.

Maynes of Manchester operated a number of ex-West Yorkshire PTE Leyland Leopards with Plaxton bodywork, including this one, GWY 692N, which was photographed at the Higginshaw Road terminus in Oldham in 1987.

Originally Ribble 401, this Leyland National was transferred to North Western as part of the privatisation of the NBC. It is seen in their bright livery while on hire to Yelloway, Rochdale, in order to bolster vehicle numbers on the latter operator's stage service commitments.

D387 VAO was an all-Leyland Royal Tiger Doyen that was originally used as a demonstrator by the manufacturer but was pretty soon snapped up by Ellen Smith of Rochdale, who operated it for some time in its demonstrator livery before repainting into fleet colours. It is seen here in their yard on Yorkshire Street.

Despite a poorly fastened skirt panel and the inevitable paper bills showing service number and destination, ex-Central SMT Leyland Leopard/Alexander Y-type OGM 604M looks quite smart as it prepares to leave Accrington on a service to Blackburn on behalf of Accrington Coachways.

Wigan Corporation 1 (EEK 1F) was a Massey-bodied Leyland Panther Cub. 22 in the Wigan fleet, it became 1676 when the undertaking was subsumed into Greater Manchester Transport. By 1981 it was in the ownership of Salford Area Health Authority, whose crest it wears where once it bore the badge depicting a Panther Cub.

Oldham's Darenettes majorette troupe used Alexander-bodied Albion Lowlander LR1 VCS 432. New in 1963 to Western SMT and later part of the Highland Scottish fleet, it is photographed in Oldham town centre.

The well-known independent Lancashire United Transport was acquired by Greater Manchester Transport in 1976 but its former vehicles were to be found in the fleets of other operators throughout the 1980s. UTE 290H, 327 in LUT's fleet, was a Bristol LH6L with attractive Northern Counties bodywork. It is seen heading south, approaching the Jubilee Bridge between Widnes and Runcorn, in the ownership of Yates's, Runcorn.

Rochdale Social Services purchased unusual bodywork on Bedford VAS5 underpinnings. GC Smith constructed the dual-door body on this 1982 example.

The only Alexander M-type motorway coach body supplied to an operator outside the Scottish Bus Group was supplied to Ribble in 1972. RTF 561L, a Leyland Leopard PUS5/4R, later found its way to Whitehead, Rochdale, who operated it on stage carriage services. Here it is in Littleborough, heading towards Rochdale.

This fine Duple Carribean-bodied Dennis Dorchester is seen in the rather incongruous surroundings of a housing estate in Milnrow, Lancashire. It was one of only five built with this combination of body and chassis, and one of two that were purchased new in 1984 by Gastonia, Cranleigh, whose livery it retains, though with the fleet name of a local operator.

In the mid-1980s, Bedford YRT/Plaxton JBY 661N was providing transport for the Saxon Martial Arts Club, Rochdale. The coach was new in 1974 to Neale, Hampton.

A not infrequent sight was a coach converted into a racing car or stock car transporter, such as this one belonging to Stu Smith. Mr Smith rightly had 'No. 1' prominently displayed on the coach, as he was a six-time World Stock Car champion. His ex-Yelloway Plaxton-bodied AEC Reliance, NDK 166G, fuels at Wardleworth, Rochdale. Ellen Smith's yard is just visible in the background.

Rigby, Eccles, was the operator of UTE 322L, a Bedford YRQ with Plaxton Panorama body that was new to Woodward, Shaw, in 1972. By the time I photographed it in 1986 in Kirkholt, Rochdale, it had acquired a Plaxton Supreme-style lower front panel.

A possibly extroverted driver has adorned the windscreen of D85 UCK, a 1986 Plaxton-bodied Leyland Tiger, with a cheery message. Walls of Wigan had only recently taken delivery of the coach when I photographed it in Leigh.

The established coach operator Smith-Shearings took up local bus services in the wake of deregulation. One of the ex GMPTE Leyland Nationals drafted in was 51 (RBU 171R), which is seen here in Bury Interchange.

Another non-PSV of interest is UTE 902H, a rare all-Seddon Pennine 4. New to Hawker Siddeley Aviation in 1969, by 1986 it had been converted to a mobile home. It is seen here in Wardleworth, Rochdale.

Healing's, Oldham, purchased this Duple Caribbean-bodied DAF MB 200 in 1984. They got good service from it, finally disposing of it in 2003.

Routemasters are not a bus associated with Lancashire. RM 1767 (767 DYE) was bought from London by the Winged Fellowship, London, in 1985 and was transferred to their Southport operation the following year, when I photographed it outside Rochdale Town Hall. The Winged Fellowship, now known as Revitalise, provide respite care in a holiday setting for disabled people and their carers.

Oldham Social Services were the owner of this unusual Plaxton Paramount-bodied Bedford VAS5, D755 LRJ. Very few VAS5/PJKs received Paramount bodies; later examples constructed by Plaxton had the Supreme body.

Pickup, Norden, acquired B287 KRW, a Leyland-bodied Royal Tiger, in 1985. It is seen here in a rather damp Rochdale town centre. This vehicle was intended to have chassis number RTC 0013, but perhaps for reasons of superstition was given chassis number RTC 0012A.

Registration number 522 CTF was first applied to a Weyman-bodied Leyland Olympian saloon that was purchased in 1957 by Fishwick, Leyland. In this 1986 shot it is associated with this Duple Dominant-bodied Leyland Tiger of Bywater, Rochdale, photographed behind what was then the Co-op superstore in the town centre. The building later became a bingo hall. The number is still in use at the time of writing, but is now attached to a 1995 Plaxton-bodied Volvo B10M.

Mercer's, Longridge, operated this much-travelled Leyland National. New to London Country in 1973 as LNC39, it was later sold to Hastings & District. It then spent some time north of the border after deregulation on loan to Eastern Scottish from Ensign (dealer) before coming back south again to Mercer's. Here it exits Preston bus station in 1986.

At first glance this is an example of the typical NBC Bristol LH/ECW combination; however, this bus was ordered not by them but by Wigan Corporation. One of six in the batch, by the time it was delivered Wigan Corporation buses had become part of the GMPTE fleet. This was also one of the last LHs to feature the flat front screen instead of the curved style that was by then standard. Long out of PSV use, it is seen in a car park in Leigh in 1986.

Another ex-municipal oddity was SUA 301M. The solitary Leyland National delivered to Leeds City Transport, it was transferred to the successor West Yorkshire PTE fleet. Later in life West Yorkshire PTE fitted a wheelchair lift, and it subsequently crossed the Pennines to join Oldham Community Transport. It is photographed in their ownership in Smallbridge.

The first Wright Contour coach to be registered was XNT 141Y, a 12-metre example on a Bedford YNT chassis. It was new in 1983 to Whittle, Highley. Bywater of Rochdale acquired it in 1985 when it was registered UAB 586Y.

Bu-Val also operated this attractive little Bedford J2 with Plaxton bodywork. It is seen parked in their lay-over area near Rochdale town centre.

Lancaster City Transport 109 (PRA 109R) is seen well outside its operator's previously traditional operating area, in Kendal, Cumbria. The Alexander T-type-bodied Leyland Leopard was new to Trent. It later passed through Stagecoach hands and is now preserved in the livery of Whites of Calvert.

Booth (Lyntown Bus Company), Eccles, WSV 550, ex-YVF 731J, a Bristol RELL 6G with ECW bodywork, heads through Manchester. The bus came to them from Eastern Counties via Cambus. Though the bus has long since been scrapped, the registration lives on with Go Goodwin, Eccles; at the time of writing it is carried by a Wright Cadet-bodied VDL SB120.

Lyntown Bus Company 10 (YFM 281L), an ex-Crosville RELL6G/ECW, passes a GMPTE Dennis Domino and a Renault, both of which were bodied by Northern Counties.

Bu-Val also operated this Plaxton Derwent-bodied Ford R1014. New in 1976 to Alder Valley, it was sold later to Rennies, Dunfermline. It was taken in part-exchange by Whitehead, Rochdale, for the ex-Ribble M-type Leopard pictured earlier and then passed to Bu-Val. Here it exits Rochdale bus station en route to Littleborough.

Accrington Coachways competed with other operators on the busy Accrington–Blackburn corridor in the period after deregulation. Ex-Ribble XTF812L, a Duple Dominant-bodied Leyland Leopard PSU3B/4R, unloads at Accrington bus station.

Pilkington, Accrington, operated this Duple Dominant-bodied Bedford VAS5, which was new to Esk Valley, Edinburgh. It is seen here in Accrington as one of the local municipal operator's East Lancs-bodied Dennis Dominators keeps close tabs on it.

A common criticism levelled at bus operators in the latter half of the 1980s was that the destination was only displayed as a scrawl on a piece of cardboard behind the windscreen, if it appeared at all. No such accusation could be justified in the case of Pilkington's URR 197G, a Bedford VAM with Plaxton bodywork, of 1969, which is seen in Accrington in 1987.

Another Plaxton of 1969 vintage, this time on an AEC Reliance chassis, Abbott's, Blackpool, OFV 467G turns out of Norton Street coach station, Manchester, heading for the Lancashire coast. This coach has spent many years after sale by Abbot's in the ownership of Kidswheels, a charity in Liverpool.

NMB 71P was a Leyland Leopard with an unusual single-deck Northern Counties body and was new to Chester in 1971. In the mid-1980s it was working for Bu-Val, Rochdale, and is seen here in Littleborough while heading up to Shore, a village that, despite its name, was adjacent to no large body of water.

R&J Coaches of Heywood were the operators of this Plaxton-bodied Leyland Leopard, which was new to Southdown. It is parked outside Entwistle Road Baths, Ochdake.

Northern Counties-bodied Renault S56 minibus E386 CNE was ordered by Fylde but early on was operated on loan to Bu-Val, Rochdale. Begrimed in the dirt of a Lancashire rainstorm, it awaits service at Rochdale bus station.

F516 OKV was an unusual Talbot Pullman six-wheel minibus demonstrator, which is seen here on loan to Bu-Val, Rochdale.

Whitehead, Rochdale, operated under the fleet name Sports Tours. Their sticker is in the windscreen of their recently acquired Alexander T-type-bodied Seddon Pennine VII, with the houses of the Belfield estate in the background. JSF 907T was new to Scottish Omnibuses and was transferred to Central SMT with Airdrie garage in 1985.

To operate services gained on deregulation, Bu-Val of Smithy Bridge purchased a number of Northern Counties-bodied Iveco 49.10 minibuses, such as this one, E186 CNE. It emerges from the low railway bridge over New Barn Lane, Rochdale.

Shearings' intake of new service buses in 1989 included 50 (F50 ENF), which sported a combination of Leyland Tiger and Alexander (Belfast) bodywork rarely seen outside Northern Ireland. It wears the Anybus livery that was used to promote a ticket that could be used on services provided by a number of operators in Greater Manchester.